I AM GRAVITY

Written by **Henry Herz**

Illustrated by **Mercè López**

TILBURY HOUSE
PUBLISHERS

Library of Congress Cataloging-in-Publication Data

Names: Herz, Henry, author. | López Arnabat, Mercè, illustrator.
Title: I am gravity / written by Henry Herz ; illustrated by Mercè López.
Description: [Ann Arbor] : Tilbury House Publishers, [2024] | Audience:
    Ages 6-9 | Summary: "Explore the amazing feats of gravity! Told in
    lyrical, riddling first-person narrative, Gravity boasts of its
    essential role in life as we know it. Back matter about the science of
    gravity and major historical discoveries enhances the book for STEM
    learning"-- Provided by publisher.
Identifiers: LCCN 2023045388 | ISBN 9781668936849 (hardcover)
Subjects: LCSH: Gravity--Juvenile literature.
Classification: LCC QC178 .H397 2024 | DDC 531/.14--dc23/eng/20231129
LC record available at https://lccn.loc.gov/2023045388

an imprint of
Cherry Lake Publishing Group
2395 South Huron Parkway, Suite 200
Ann Arbor, MI 48104
www.tilburyhouse.com

Printed and bound in South Korea

10 9 8 7 6 5 4 3 2 1

To my wife, my sons, and
the Author of all things.
—Henry Herz

To Antonia,
"I hug you forever."
—Mercè López

I am gravity.

You feel me but cannot see me. I reach
everywhere, touching everything . . .

...a butterfly landing on your outstretched palm,
a whale diving deep, the moon far above

I gather hydrogen clouds in the vast, cold remoteness of space, compressing them into giant swirling knots. I squeeze so fiercely that hydrogen can fuse into helium, forging stars.
There is light. Far-flung lamps
twinkle in the night sky.

Over millions of years, I pack molecules into planets—
gaseous globes like Jupiter and rocky balls like Earth.

I pinch so powerfully that their cores can become as hot as the sun's surface. I have existed since the dawn of time.

I am gravity.

I tug on everything—dandelion puffs
and mighty galaxies. I am stubborn—
the bigger things are, the harder I pull.

My grip even warps the path of light around stars and planets.

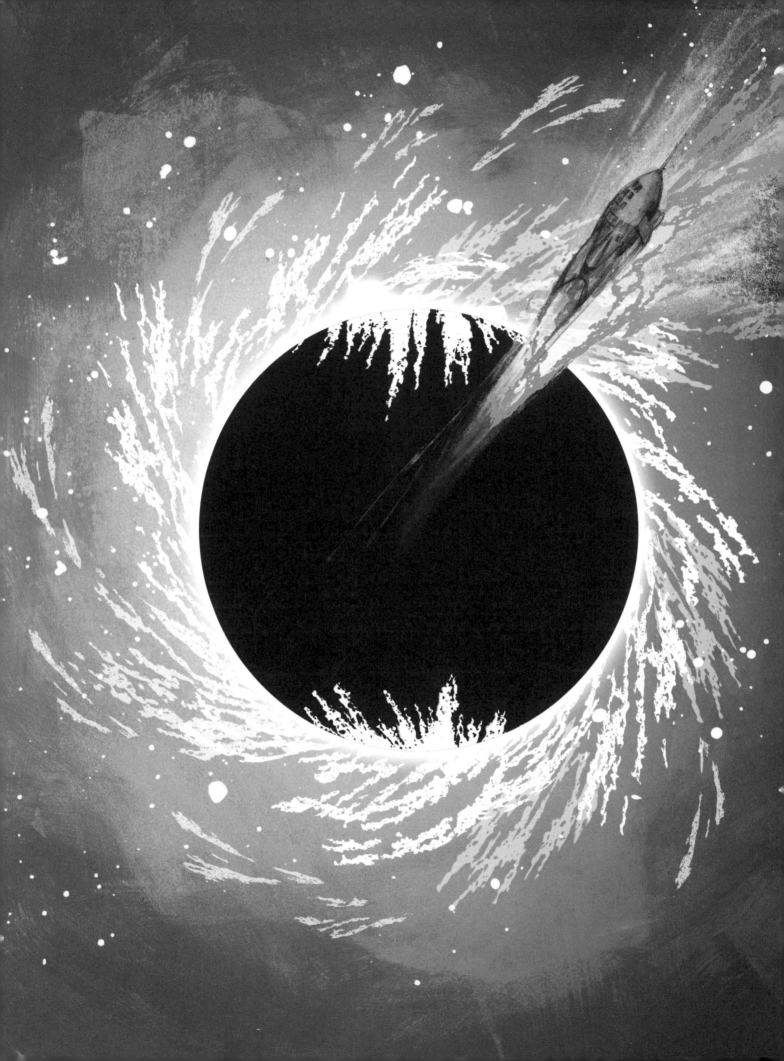

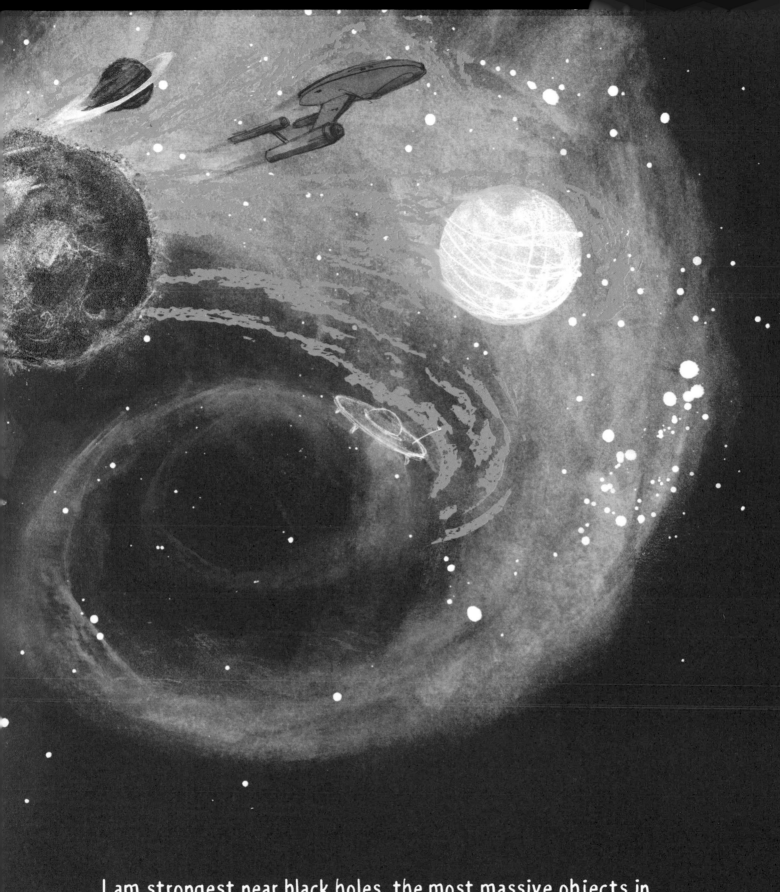

I am strongest near black holes, the most massive objects in
the universe. I feed them anything that wanders too close.
Each meal makes them more massive . . . and greedier.

The greater the distance, the weaker my grasp.
Stars are huge, but so far away that I do not draw
you into the heavens. Still, I have the strength to
hold the Milky Way together—and I never, ever tire.

I am gravity.

My grip twirls Earth at just the right
distance from the sun to keep you warm.

I tether the moon to the Earth. High tide.
Low tide. I wave to you with the oceans.

Thanks to me, water and air wrap Earth in a
life-giving bubble instead of drifting away.

The winds blow because
I hold colder air down.

I make rain fall and smoke rise.

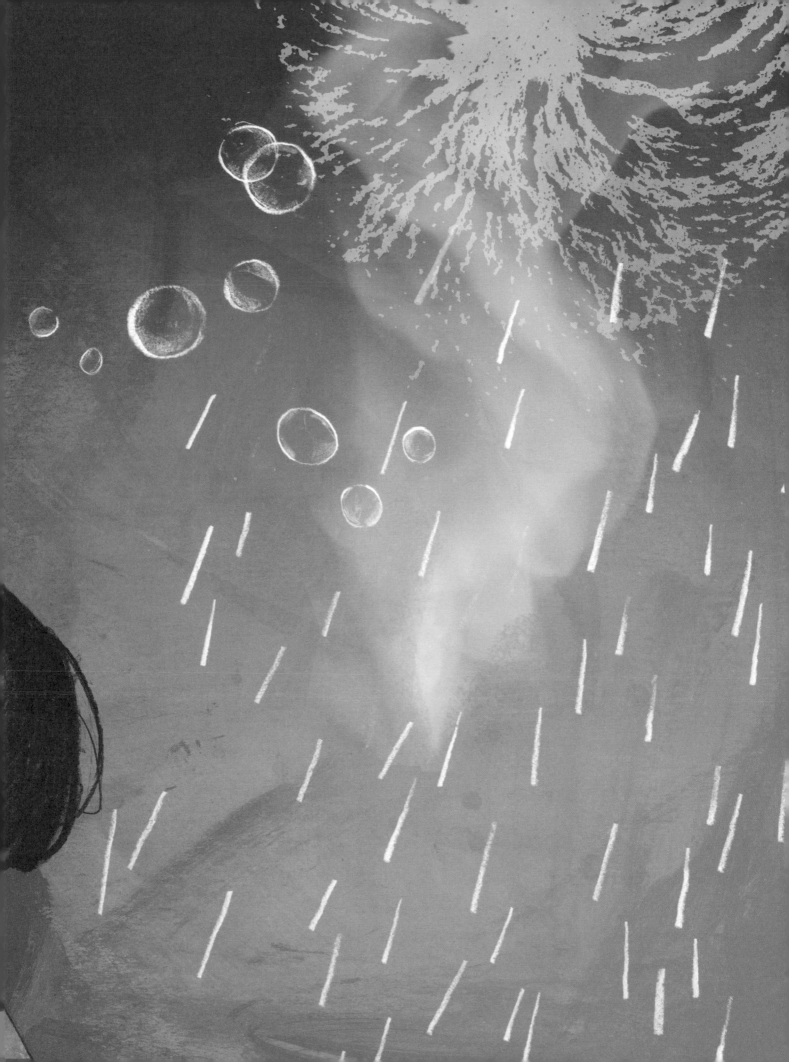

My embrace is tight enough that you
don't float like a balloon, but loose enough
that you can run and leap and play.

I am gravity.

The outward push of a star's burning heart balances my inward pull.

Stars withstand my squeezing for billions of years . . . but not forever.

When the fuel in a star's core
is used up, my grip crushes it.

Sometimes the collapse blasts
outward in all directions.

Shock waves ripple through clouds of
hydrogen drifting in the suddenly bright void.

Again I gather swirling molecules, squeezing
until new stars twinkle in the heavens.

I hug you forever.

I am gravity.

Author Notes for Curious Readers

Who would expect that something invisible could so profoundly affect us? Or that it would be far more complex than first envisioned? The universe as we know it is shaped by gravity. Stars and planets could not exist without gravity and neither could we.

Mass describes how much matter an object has. It represents an object's resistance to being moved. Your mass stays the same no matter where you are. Weight, on the other hand, measures how powerfully gravity acts upon you. That's why you'd weigh more on Jupiter, which has stronger gravity, than on Earth.

In 1687, Sir Isaac Newton proposed his law of universal gravitation. It stated that each particle in the universe attracts every other particle with a force that is proportional to the product of their masses. But the attraction is also *inversely* proportional to the square of the distance between their centers. So every planet exerts a force on you, but only Earth is close enough to produce a noticeable effect. This theory did an excellent job of describing what could be observed. Until . . .

In 1915, Albert Einstein's general theory of relativity provided a more accurate description of gravity. He added time to width, length, and height as a fourth dimension of what he called space-time. Space-time is the fabric of the universe. Mass warps space-time similar to the way standing on a trampoline warps its surface. If a ball is rolled on the trampoline, it will curve toward you. Stars and planets bend space-time in the same way.

Now hold on to your brain for this next part. Einstein also theorized that even light warps when traveling near large masses like stars. His mind-bending claim was first confirmed by scientific experiment in 1919. Black holes are so massive that objects and even light that comes close (within the "event horizon") get sucked inside by gravity, never to escape.

Newton thought gravity was an instantaneous force. Einstein replied, "No way, dude." Well, he didn't really say that. Instead Einstein developed the concept of gravitational waves that convey the effects of gravity between objects at the speed of light. That's mighty fast—186,000 miles per second—but not instantaneous. In 2015, scientists directly detected gravitational waves, proving Einstein right again.

Gravity is essential for planet and star formation. Over millions of years, gas and dust clump together—the bigger the clump, the more it attracts additional atoms. With enough mass, the material collapses under its own gravity. As the pressure continues to increase, the temperature of the core rises until it gets so hot that fusion reactions begin—a star is born. Hydrogen fuses to form helium. More fusion creates heavier elements. The outward pressure from fusion counteracts the inward pull of gravity.

Once a star's fuel is used up, gravity takes over. If the star is big enough, its rapid collapse creates shock waves, blasting the outer part of the star into space. Some of that debris may eventually collide with interstellar molecules to form new stars and planets. Hold on to your brain again. The heavier elements that make up your body—like carbon, nitrogen, silicon, oxygen, and iron—were originally forged within the cores of stars. You are literally made of stardust!

Gravity keeps us alive, too. It maintains Earth's orbit around the sun by counteracting the outward centrifugal force generated by Earth's motion. Without the sun's gravity, Earth would be flung into the cold of space. Thanks, gravity!

Henry Herz (San Diego, California) writes fantasy, science fiction, and nonfiction. He is the author of numerous short stories and eleven picture books, including *I Am Smoke*, which earned a *Kirkus* starred review, was an ALA Notable Children's Book, and was listed in *School Library Journal*'s Most Astonishingly Unconventional Children's Books of 2021 and the New York Public Library's Best Books for Kids. He holds a BS in engineering from Cornell, an MS in engineering from George Washington University, and an MA in political science from Georgetown University.

Mercè López (Barcelona, Spain) graduated from Llotja School of Art in Barcelona and has illustrated around fifteen children's books for Spanish and international book publishers. She has also illustrated for design, theater, and film. She is the illustrator of *I Am Smoke* and won the 2022 Lazarillo Award for *Montañas*, together with author Javier Bermúdez. Her 2019 title, *Lion of the Sky: Haiku for All Seasons* by Laura Purdie Salas, received multiple starred reviews and was named a *BCCB* Gryphon Honor Book, an NCTE Notable Poetry Book, a *Kirkus* Best Picture Book, and a *Parents* magazine Best Children's Book, among other accolades.